The Kingdom of Bloom

Written by Kerrie Shanahan

Illustrated by Ian Forss

Flying Start
to Literacy®

Contents

Chapter 1:
A problem in the kingdom

Once there was a beautiful palace,
high on a hill in the Kingdom of Bloom.
It was surrounded by green gardens,
singing birds and clean streams.

In the palace lived the king and his family.
They had everything they could ever want
and they were all very happy.

The Director of Fun made sure that the king
was busy having fun – all day, every day.

But, outside the palace walls, it was very different. There were no green gardens. There were no singing birds and no clean streams.

The Kingdom of Bloom was dirty.
The sun was hidden behind grey clouds.
The streams were dirty, the plants were brown and all the people were unhappy.

6

No one knew what to do about all the rubbish and pollution. But Marco had an idea.

Marco lived in Budsville, the dirtiest, most polluted town in the whole kingdom. He knew that things had to change.

"If the king only knew what it was really like in his kingdom," he said, "we might be able to fix this mess!"

So he wrote a letter to the king.

When the king received Marco's letter, he was shocked.

"A boy called Marco says that the Kingdom of Bloom is filthy," said the king. "He says it is full of rubbish and weeds and pollution.   Is this true?"

"Of course there's some rubbish," said the
Director of Fun.   "Don't worry about it.
Now, let's do something fun."

"Stop," said the king.   "No more fun until
I sort this out!   I will go and see for myself."

So the king went outside the palace to see
the Kingdom of Bloom.

Chapter 2:
A shock for the king

When the king saw all the pollution, he was shocked and angry.

"How did this happen?" he asked. "How did my beautiful kingdom become so polluted? And what can I do to fix it?"

The king thought and thought.

"I know," he said at last. "I will hold
a competition. I will give the people six
months to clean up their own towns. Then
I will choose the tidiest town! The prize
for the winning town will be a beautiful
green garden full of flowers and
singing birds."

All the people in the kingdom were excited about the competition and began to clean up their towns.

They swept the streets and washed walls. They picked up rubbish and recycled paper, cans and glass. They planted gardens and cleaned up creeks.

Throughout the kingdom, the towns were
beginning to look cleaner.

Chapter 3:

A slow start in Budsville

But, in Budsville, things were different.

"We can't win this competition," the people said. "Look at this place. How can we fix such a huge problem? It's pointless! Budsville will never be clean!"

"Wait," said Marco. "We can do it if we work together. Let's start by cleaning up the town square. Meet me there tomorrow morning. If we all work together, we can make a difference."

But no one was listening to Marco.

The next morning, Marco arrived early at the town square. He scrubbed the steps and pulled out weeds. He painted the seats and planted new plants.

As he was working, some people stopped to help. Then some more people stopped to help. Soon, there were lots of people helping Marco.

By the end of the day, the town square
was clean!

"Next, we will clean up the lake,"
said Marco. "Tell your family and friends."

Lots of people came to help Marco
clean up the lake.

People picked up rubbish from the edge of
the lake. They pulled out weeds and
planted new plants.

News spread about how good the lake looked. From then on, every weekend, more and more people helped Marco to clean up Budsville.

Chapter 4:
The winner is . . .

The time came for the king to choose a winner of the tidiest town competition. He went to every town in his kingdom and was very impressed with what he saw.

But, when he got to Budsville, he was
amazed! The dirtiest, smelliest town was
now neat and clean. There were new bins
and recycling stations, and flowers were
blooming everywhere.

"This is by far the tidiest town," declared
the king. "Budsville is the winner of the
competition."

The people of Budsville clapped and cheered.

"We must never let our kingdom become
polluted again," said the king. "And, to
make sure that it stays neat and clean,
I want Marco to become the Director
for the Environment."

From that day on, the king and all the
people in the kingdom lived happily
ever after in the beautiful and clean
Kingdom of Bloom!

A note from the author

When I was a young child, I lived in a small country town. I remember when our town was awarded the title of "Tidiest Town". All the students at my school were very excited, and the award gave our town a sense of community and a feeling of pride. This event stuck in my mind and was the spark I used when I began to write *The Kingdom of Bloom*.

I believe that one person can make a difference – just like Marco did in Budsville. So, if you have an idea or a plan, then go for it! Sometimes, the smallest ideas end up growing into something amazing!